SUPER TALENTED DOGS

Written by Annabel Griffin   Illustrated by Marina Halak

Copyright © 2024 Hungry Tomato Ltd

First published in 2024 by Hungry Tomato Ltd
F15, Old Bakery Studios, Blewetts Wharf, Malpas Road, Truro, Cornwall,
TR1 1QH, UK.

No part of this publication may be reproduced, stored in a retrieval system, or transmitted in any form or by any means, electronic, mechanical, photocopying, recording, or otherwise, without prior written permission of the copyright owner.

A CIP catalogue record for this book is available from the British Library.

ISBN 9781916598744

Printed in China

Discover more at
www.hungrytomato.com

CONTENTS

The World of Dogs	4
Breed Groups	6
Super Talented Dogs	8
Super Sniffers	9
Speedy Dogs	14
Little Diggers	18
Fetch!	20
Clever Climbers	22
What's That Dog?	24
Spot the Dog	26
Skills to the Test	28
Glossary	30
Index	31

Words in **BOLD** can be found in the glossary.

THE WORLD OF DOGS

Get ready to explore the wonderful world of super talented dogs! From super sniffers to clever climbers, there are so many different types of brilliant dogs to discover.

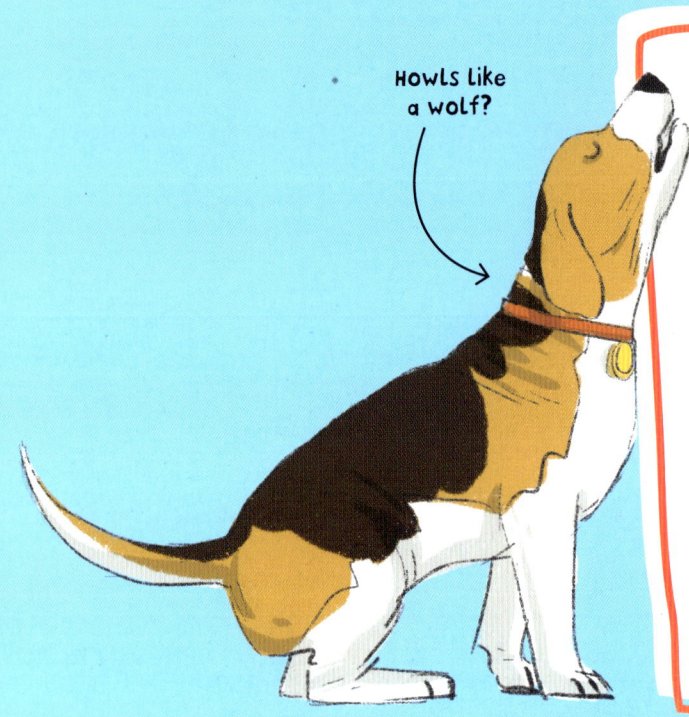

Howls like a wolf?

WHERE DO DOGS COME FROM?

Believe it or not, all dogs are **descendants** of ancient wolves. The details of how and when wolves became dogs are still quite foggy, but it likely started when humans began to **domesticate** and train wolves, at least 14,000 years ago. Today, dogs can be found all over the world.

WHAT IS A BREED?

A breed is a particular group of dogs that all share the same (or very similar) appearance and **characteristics**, making them easy to identify. There are hundreds of different breeds, and they can vary wildly in size, shape, hairiness, and personality.

Not all dogs belong to a specific breed. Some dogs, known as mutts or mongrels, are a mixture of lots of different breeds. They can make fantastic pets, and can often be found looking for a loving home at rescue or **rehoming shelters.**

Big and small, they've got it all!

GETTING A DOG?

Maybe you already have a dog in your family, or maybe you'd like to in the future. Owning a dog can be fun and rewarding, but it's also a big responsibility. Some dogs need a lot of space, time and attention. Before buying or **adopting** a dog, you should always carefully research their breed and think about whether you are able to give them everything they need to be happy.

Look at those puppy eyes!

BREED GROUPS

Dog breeds are often arranged into seven different groups, that are loosely based on the jobs that they were originally bred to do.

SPORTING GROUP

Also known as gundogs, these dogs were originally bred to help hunters retrieve birds.

NON-SPORTING GROUP

This is the group for dogs that don't fit into any of the other groups, so they are quite a mixed bunch!

TERRIER GROUP

This group were originally bred to hunt burrowing animals, such as rats, rabbits, foxes, and badgers. Most of them have "terrier" as part of their name.

WORKING GROUP

Dogs in this group were originally bred to perform practical tasks, such as pulling sleds and carts. They were also often used as watchdogs. They are usually large dogs.

SIGHTHOUNDS
These dogs are usually long, lean and very fast.

SCENT HOUNDS
These dogs have droopy ears and powerful noses.

HOUND GROUP

Hounds were bred for their sense of smell or sight, and were usually used for hunting. They can be split into two sub-groups: sighthounds and scent hounds.

HERDING GROUP

This group includes dogs that were bred to work on farms; herding and guarding livestock, such as sheep and cows.

TOY GROUP

Tiny breeds that are small enough to sit in your lap fall into this group. They are bred mostly as pets and companions.

SUPER TALENTED DOGS

There are some really talented dogs out there! While all dogs are amazing, some breeds are particularly skilled at certain things. Some have incredible noses, capable of sniffing out scents from miles away. Others are incredibly speedy, great at fetch, or clever climbers. Many of these skills are useful for performing particular jobs or tasks, but they can also be a lot of fun!

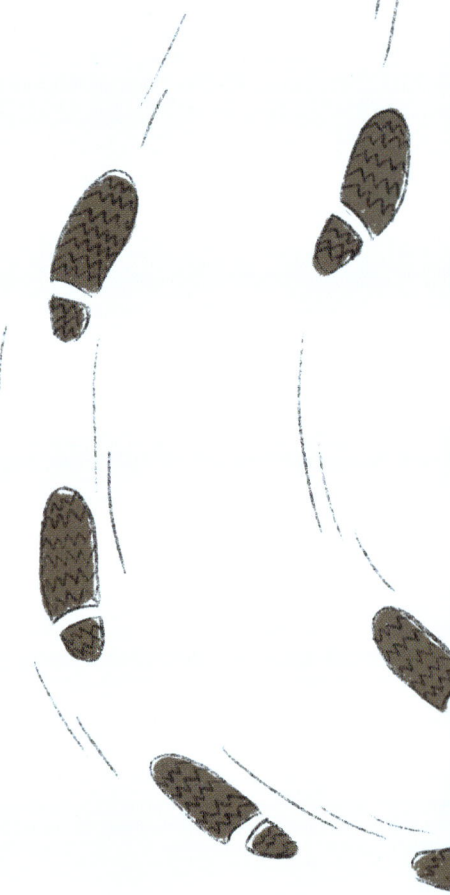

SUPER SNIFFERS   **9**

Bloodhound

The bloodhound has the strongest sense of smell of any dog breed. With their super noses and excellent tracking skills, they are often used by police detectives to help solve crimes and find missing people.

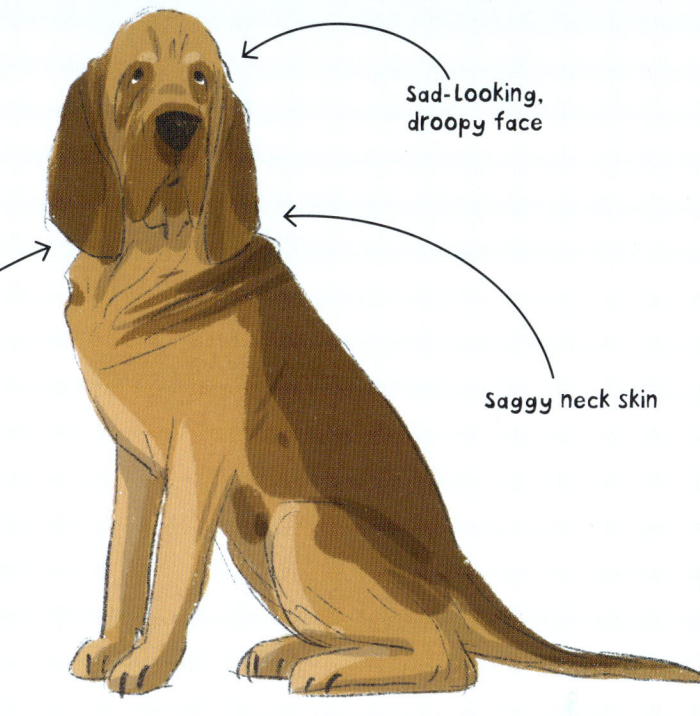

Sad-looking, droopy face

Saggy neck skin

Long, dangling ears

ORIGIN: Belgium

COAT: Short, smooth

PERSONALITY: Inquisitive

INTELLIGENCE 🐾🐾🐾

ENERGY LEVEL 🐾🐾🐾🐾

TRAINABILITY 🐾🐾🐾🐾

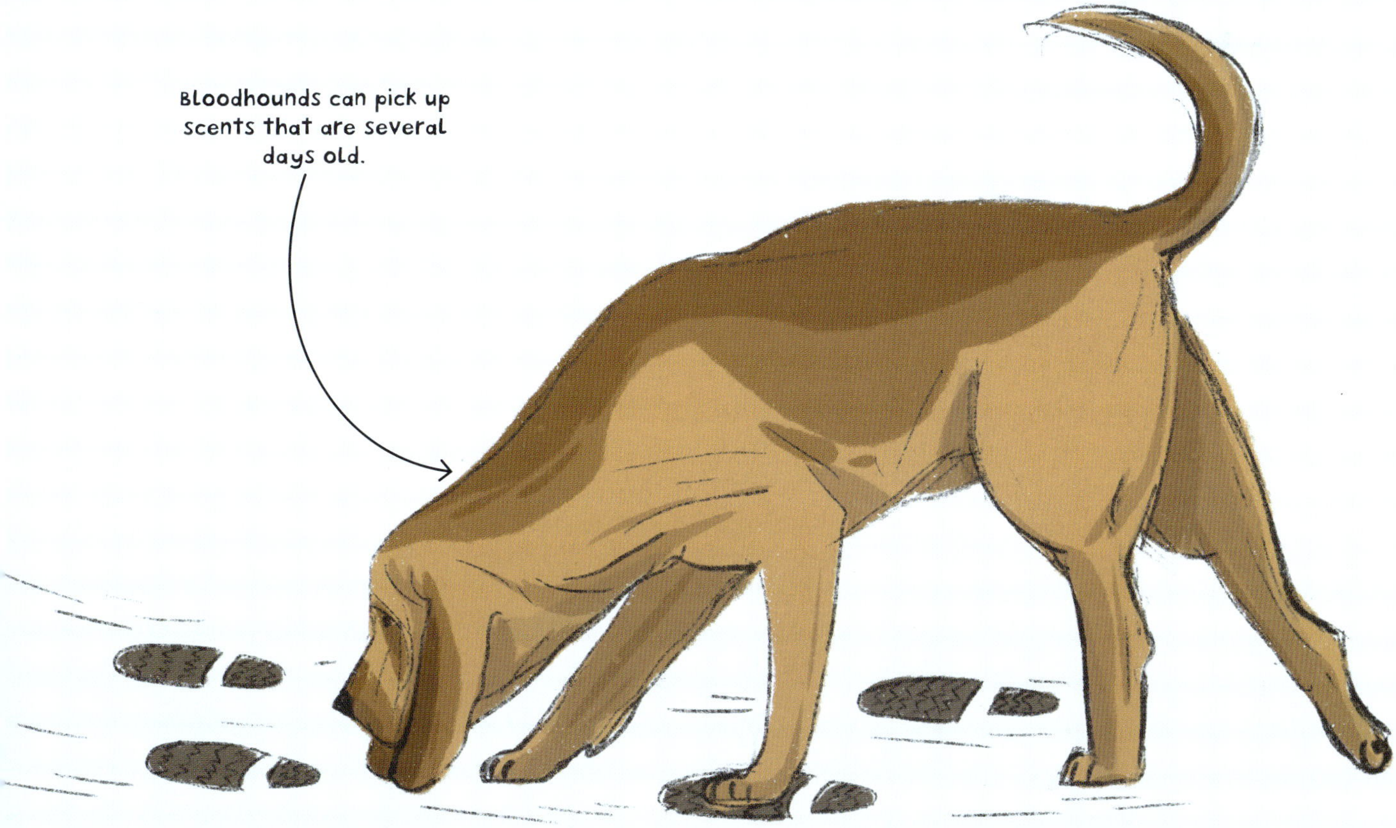

Bloodhounds can pick up scents that are several days old.

SUPER SNIFFERS

Basset Hound

The basset hound's sense of smell is second only to the bloodhound (page 9). Its long floppy ears help to trap smells and waft them towards its nose.

- Surprisingly heavy
- Resting sad face
- Droopy ears
- Stubby legs

ORIGIN: United Kingdom
COAT: Short, smooth
PERSONALITY: Friendly & easy-going

INTELLIGENCE
ENERGY LEVEL
TRAINABILITY

American Foxhound

These dogs were one of the first breeds to be developed in the United States, and were even bred by President George Washington. However, they are now one of the rarest breeds in the country.

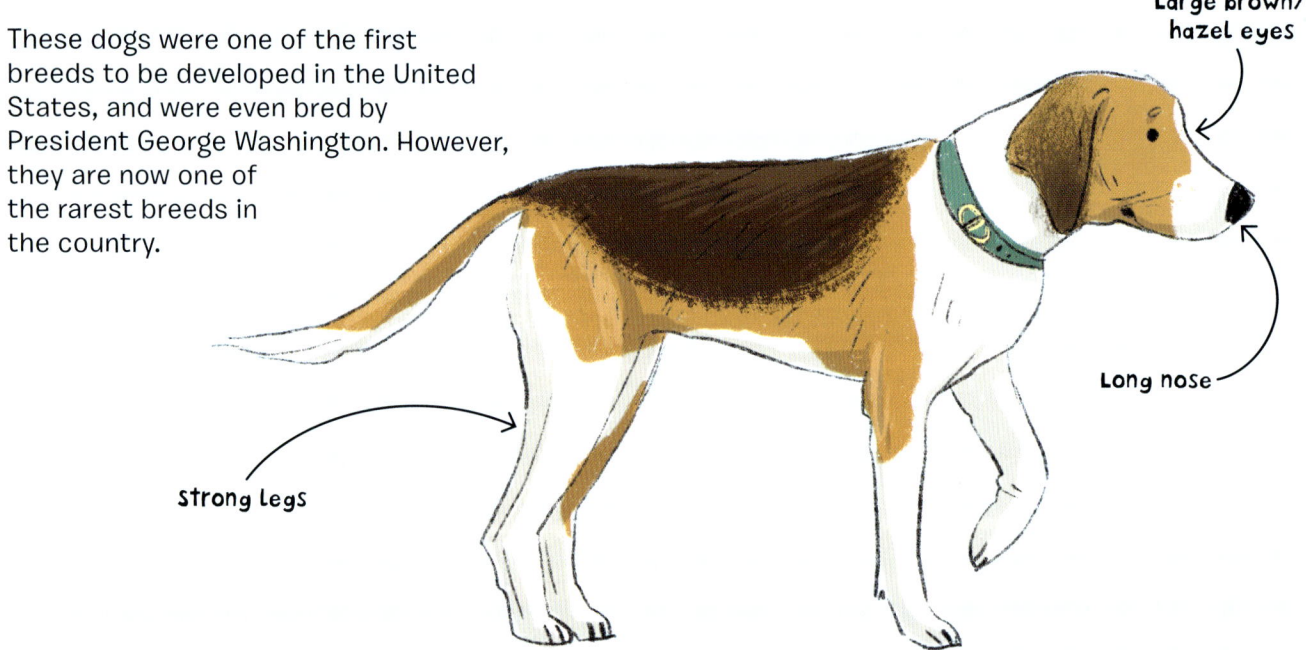

- Large brown/hazel eyes
- Long nose
- Strong legs

ORIGIN: USA
COAT: Short, smooth
PERSONALITY: Kind & gentle

INTELLIGENCE
ENERGY LEVEL
TRAINABILITY

SUPER SNIFFERS 11

Otterhound

This very rare breed was originally bred to hunt otters in medieval England. Their powerful noses can track scents through water over long distances, and they are excellent swimmers.

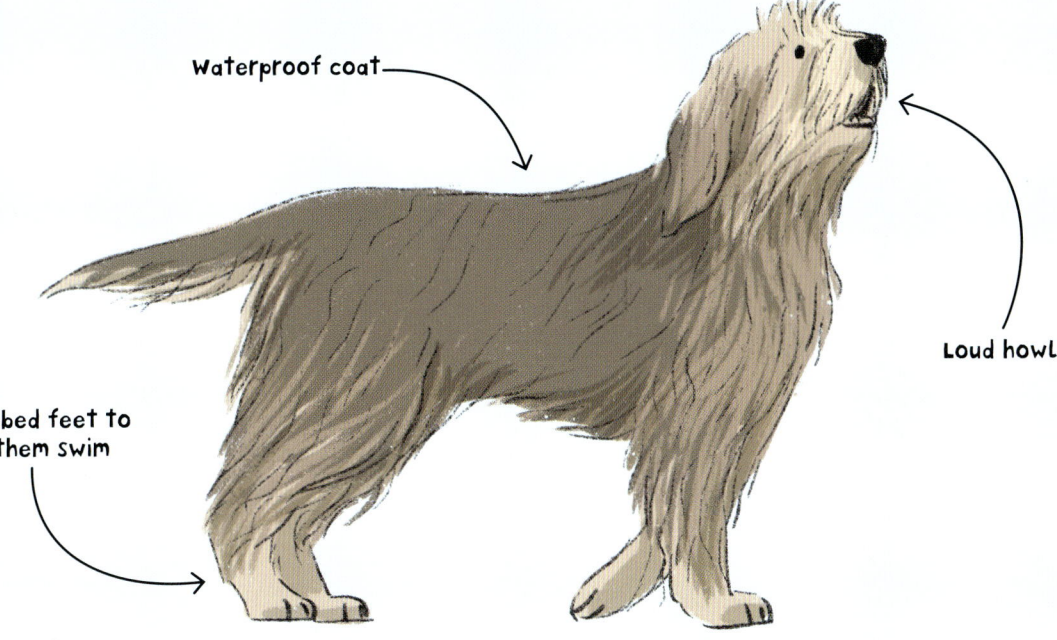

- Waterproof coat
- Loud howl
- Big webbed feet to help them swim

ORIGIN: United Kingdom
COAT: Medium-length, rough
PERSONALITY: Playful & outgoing

INTELLIGENCE 🐾🐾🐾🐾🐾
ENERGY LEVEL 🐾🐾🐾🐾🐾
TRAINABILITY 🐾🐾🐾🐾🐾

English Springer Spaniel

Springer spaniels are often trained as **detection dogs,** as they can be taught to identify and track particular smells. They also make fun-loving family pets!

- Long, wavy ears
- Full of energy
- Very waggy tail

ORIGIN: United Kingdom
COAT: Medium-length
PERSONALITY: Lively & affectionate

INTELLIGENCE 🐾🐾🐾🐾🐾
ENERGY LEVEL 🐾🐾🐾🐾🐾
TRAINABILITY 🐾🐾🐾🐾🐾

12 SUPER SNIFFERS

Beagle

These small hounds were first bred for hunting, but have also become popular pets. They are sometimes used as detection dogs, trained to sniff out drugs, explosives, and other items.

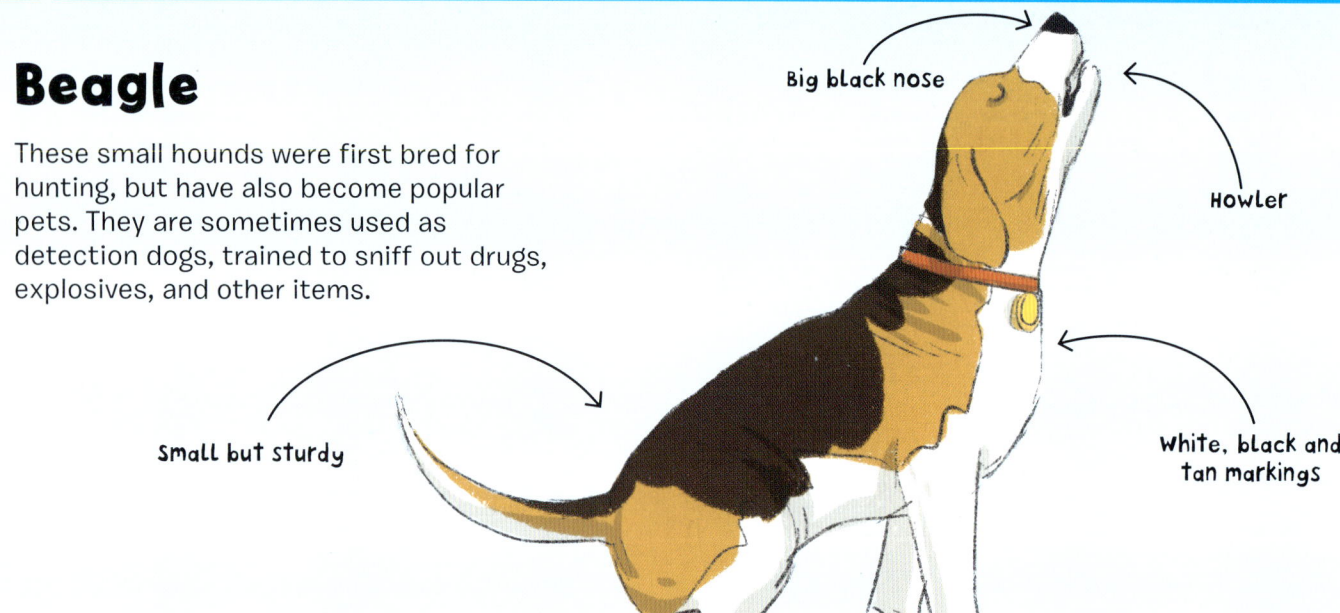

Big black nose
Howler
White, black and tan markings
Small but sturdy

ORIGIN: United Kingdom
COAT: Short, smooth
PERSONALITY: Friendly and curious

INTELLIGENCE
ENERGY LEVEL
TRAINABILITY

Bluetick Coonhound

Bred to sniff out raccoons and opossums, these hounds love to hunt and chase in the great outdoors. Even though they have lots of energy when out tracking, they also love a good nap!

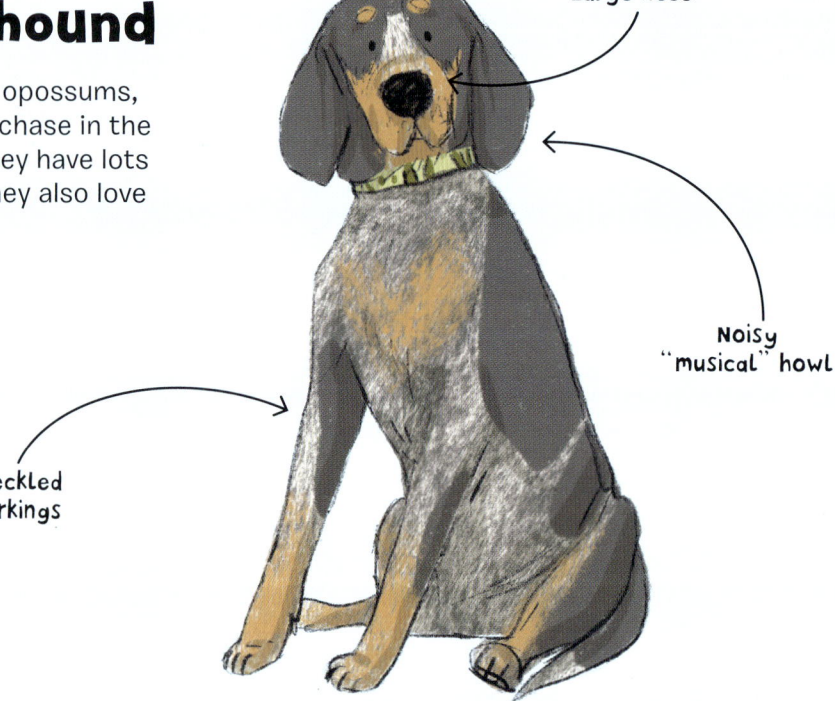

Large nose
Noisy "musical" howl
Speckled markings

ORIGIN: USA
COAT: Short, smooth
PERSONALITY: Friendly and curious

INTELLIGENCE
ENERGY LEVEL
TRAINABILITY

SUPER SNIFFERS 13

Lagotto Romagnolo

These adorable curly-coated pups are known for making great **truffle** hounds in Italy. Their strong sense of smell helps them to sniff out rare, valuable truffles buried in the ground.

Face covered in curls

Makes you want to give it a big cuddle!

Teddy bear looks

ORIGIN: Italy
COAT: Medium-length, curly
PERSONALITY: Affectionate and lively

INTELLIGENCE
ENERGY LEVEL
TRAINABILITY

Belgian Malinois

The Malinois is a short-haired variety of Belgian shepherd. They are very intelligent, easy to train and have a great sense of smell, so are often used for detection and search-and-rescue work.

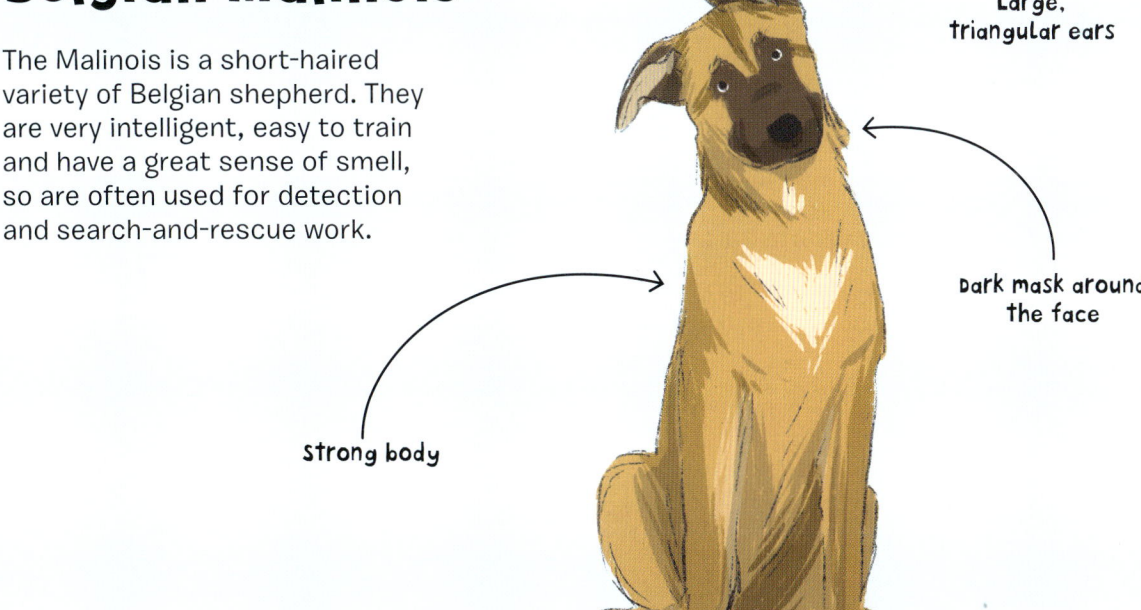

Large, triangular ears

Dark mask around the face

Strong body

ORIGIN: Belgium
COAT: Short, smooth
PERSONALITY: Confident & hard-working

INTELLIGENCE
ENERGY LEVEL
TRAINABILITY

SPEEDY DOGS

Greyhound

These dogs were born to run! Capable of reaching 45 mph (72 km/h), they win the race for fastest breed in the world.

They are an old breed that were originally bred for hunting, but are now better known as racing dogs.

Long neck

ORIGIN: Belgium

COAT: Short, smooth

PERSONALITY: Gentle and sensitive

INTELLIGENCE

ENERGY LEVEL

TRAINABILITY

Slim, athletic body

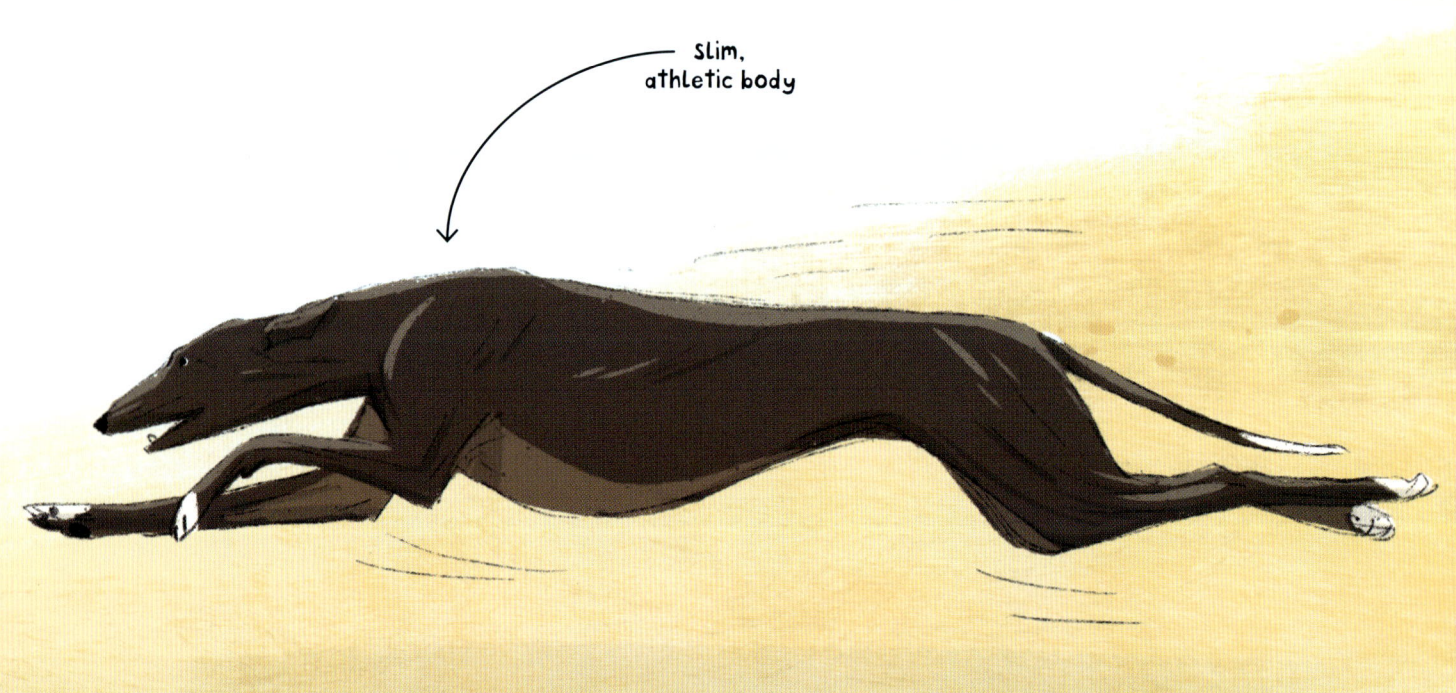

SPEEDY DOGS

Even though they are super speedy, greyhounds only need short daily bursts of exercise. Afterwards, they will happily spend the rest of their time lounging around and snoozing.

16 SPEEDY DOGS

Saluki

The saluki is one of the world's oldest breeds, with a history dating back thousands of years across the Middle East, from Egypt to Iran. While the greyhound may be a speedier sprinter, the saluki is fastest over long distances. Their top speed is 43 mph (69km/h).

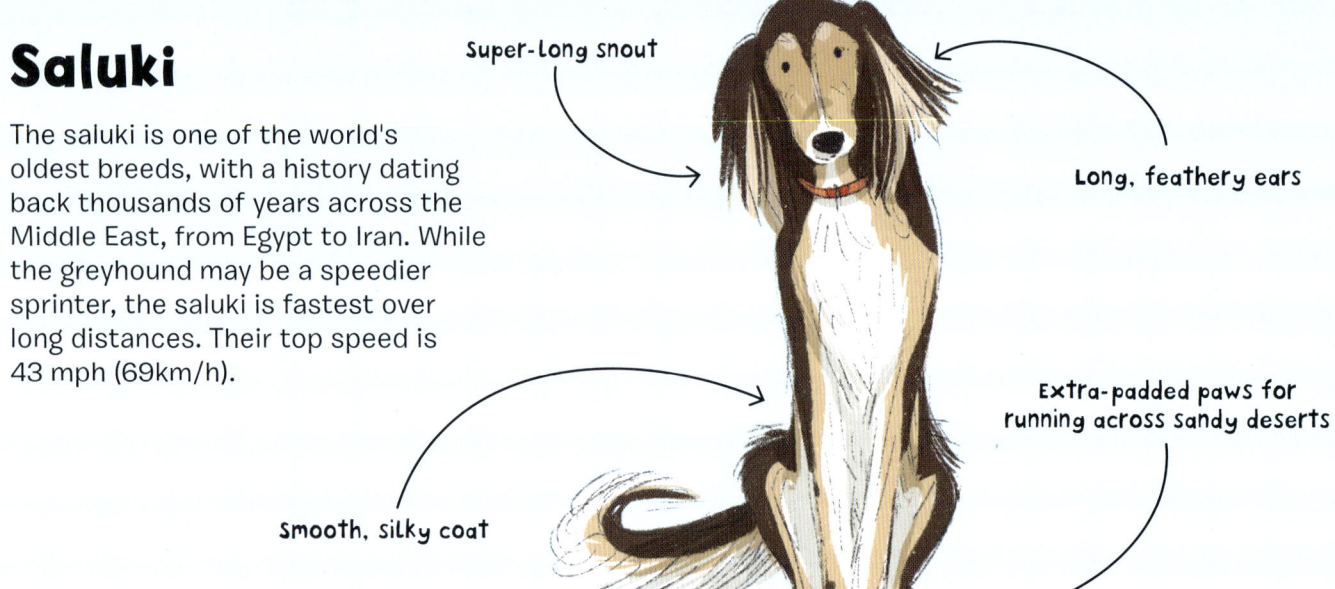

- Super-long snout
- Long, feathery ears
- Extra-padded paws for running across sandy deserts
- Smooth, silky coat

ORIGIN: Middle East (exact origin unknown)
COAT: Short, smooth
PERSONALITY: Shy and independent

INTELLIGENCE: 🐾🐾🐾🐾
ENERGY LEVEL: 🐾🐾🐾🐾
TRAINABILITY: 🐾🐾🐾

Vizsla

These Hungarian hunting dogs can reach top speeds of 40 mph (64 km/h). They are also very intelligent and easy to train.

- Strong back
- Light brown nose
- Golden coat

ORIGIN: Hungary
COAT: Short, smooth
PERSONALITY: Energetic & affectionate

INTELLIGENCE: 🐾🐾🐾🐾🐾
ENERGY LEVEL: 🐾🐾🐾🐾🐾
TRAINABILITY: 🐾🐾🐾🐾🐾

SPEEDY DOGS 17

Whippet

Whippets look a lot like greyhounds (pages 14-15) but are smaller. They're also not quite as speedy, but with a top speed of 35 mph (56km/h), they are still one of the fastest dogs around!

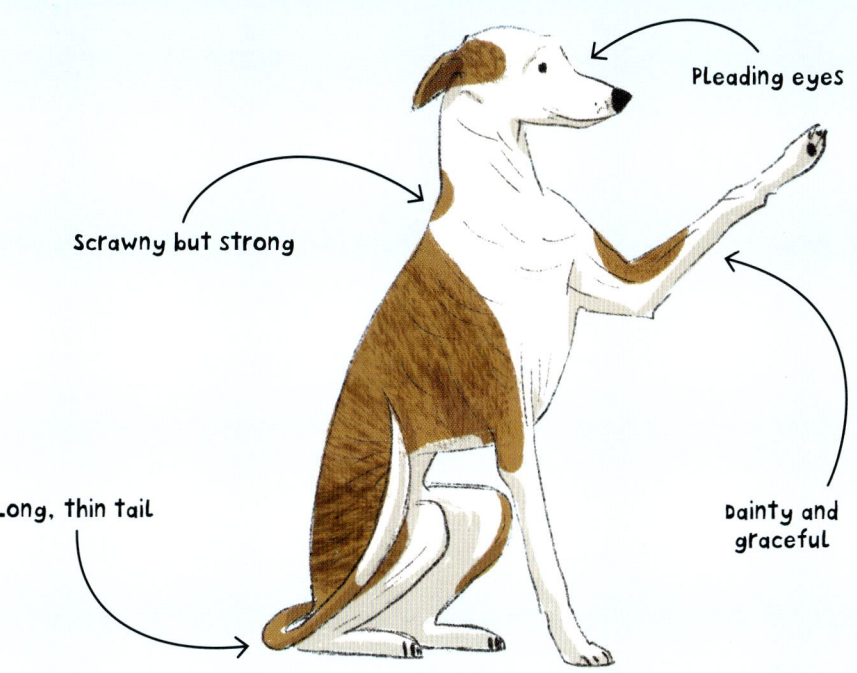

Pleading eyes
Scrawny but strong
Long, thin tail
Dainty and graceful

ORIGIN: United Kingdom
COAT: Short, smooth
PERSONALITY: Quiet and loving

INTELLIGENCE 🐾🐾🐾
ENERGY LEVEL 🐾🐾🐾🐾
TRAINABILITY 🐾🐾🐾

Jack Russell Terrier

Don't let their little legs fool you. These bouncy little terriers can reach some serious speeds! They are the fastest small breed and can reach speeds of 30 mph (48km/h).

coats can be smooth or wiry
Loves to play
Small but sturdy

ORIGIN: United Kingdom
COAT: Short, smooth or **wiry**
PERSONALITY: Feisty and lively

INTELLIGENCE 🐾🐾🐾🐾
ENERGY LEVEL 🐾🐾🐾🐾🐾
TRAINABILITY 🐾🐾🐾

18 LITTLE DIGGERS

Scottish Terrier

"Scotties" were originally bred in the Scottish Highlands. They are quick and feisty little dogs, trained to dig their way into **burrows**. Although most terriers are now kept as pets, they haven't lost their love for digging!

SMALL

ORIGIN: United Kingdom
COAT: Medium-length, wiry
PERSONALITY: Alert and territorial

INTELLIGENCE
ENERGY LEVEL
TRAINABILITY

West Highland White Terrier

Most old breeds of terrier were bred to be small enough to fit through tunnels made by burrowing animals. "Westies" are another Scottish breed. They are confident, fun-loving, and cuddly little dogs.

SMALL

ORIGIN: United Kingdom
COAT: Medium-length, thick
PERSONALITY: Playful and outgoing

INTELLIGENCE
ENERGY LEVEL
TRAINABILITY

LITTLE DIGGERS 19

Border Terrier

Border terriers love to be part of the family. They are good at **agility** and games. Their hunting instincts are strong, so they may try to chase smaller animals.

whiskery face

Longer legs than most small terriers

Short, thick tail

SMALL

ORIGIN: United Kingdom
COAT: Short, wiry
PERSONALITY: Confident and friendly

INTELLIGENCE 🐾🐾🐾🐾
ENERGY LEVEL 🐾🐾🐾
TRAINABILITY 🐾🐾🐾🐾

Wire Fox Terrier

As their name suggests, these dogs were originally bred to hunt foxes. These little dogs have very big personalities!

Handsome looking

Long head

Long legs

SMALL

ORIGIN: United Kingdom
COAT: Medium-length, wiry
PERSONALITY: Alert and adventurous

INTELLIGENCE 🐾🐾🐾🐾
ENERGY LEVEL 🐾🐾🐾🐾
TRAINABILITY 🐾🐾🐾

FETCH!

Portuguese Water Dog

These dogs are a fisherman's best friend! Traditionally, they were trained to retrieve fishing equipment from the water, herd fish into nets, and deliver messages between ships. Their "lion cut" hairdo may look weird but it was designed to keep their top half warm in cold waters, while shaving their back legs allowed for easier movement while swimming.

However you style it, their coat needs a lot of grooming!

Feathery tail

Natural swimmers

ORIGIN: Portugal
COAT: Long, curly/wavy
PERSONALITY: Clever and athletic

INTELLIGENCE
ENERGY LEVEL
TRAINABILITY

Weimaraner

This striking dog is nicknamed the "Grey Ghost". Graceful and energetic, they were bred to be brilliant retrievers, so are fantastic at fetch!

Striking, pale eyes

Shiny silver-grey coat

Sneaky mover

ORIGIN: Germany
COAT: Short, smooth
PERSONALITY: Active and playful

INTELLIGENCE
ENERGY LEVEL
TRAINABILITY

FETCH! 21

Nova Scotia Duck Tolling Retriever

These dogs are professional fetch players! They were used for an unusual type of hunting, where a hunter would play a game of fetch with their dog to try and lure in curious ducks and geese.

- Thick, waterproof coat
- Needs a catchier name!
- White chest markings
- Smallest breed of retriever

ORIGIN: United Kingdom
COAT: Short, wiry
PERSONALITY: Smart and affectionate

INTELLIGENCE
ENERGY LEVEL
TRAINABILITY

German Pointer

These outdoorsy dogs are brilliant at trailing, tracking and retrieving. They are very energetic and need lots of fresh air and exercise.

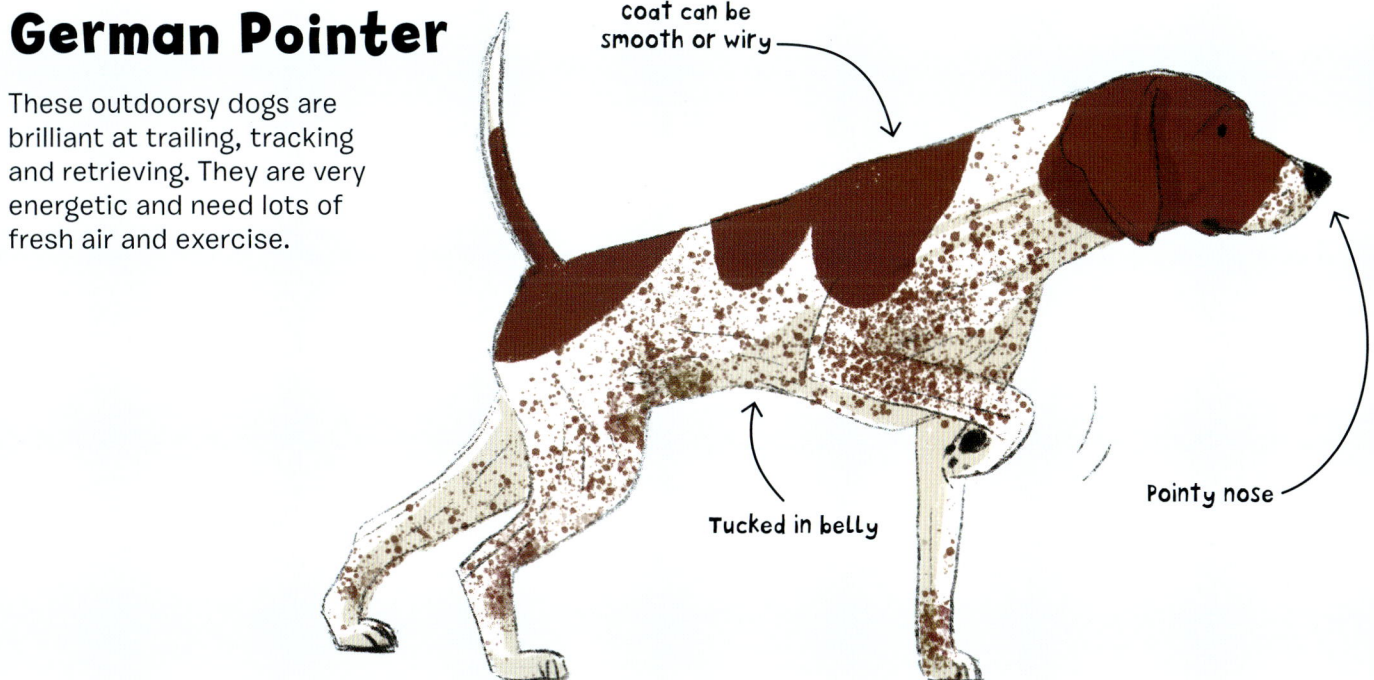

- Coat can be smooth or wiry
- Pointy nose
- Tucked in belly

ORIGIN: United Kingdom
COAT: Short, smooth or wiry
PERSONALITY: Sporty and outgoing

INTELLIGENCE
ENERGY LEVEL
TRAINABILITY

CLEVER CLIMBERS

Treeing Walker Coonhound

This breed is trained to chase raccoons up trees. Some have been known to follow them up the tree! They are energetic and playful dogs, but they can bark a lot.

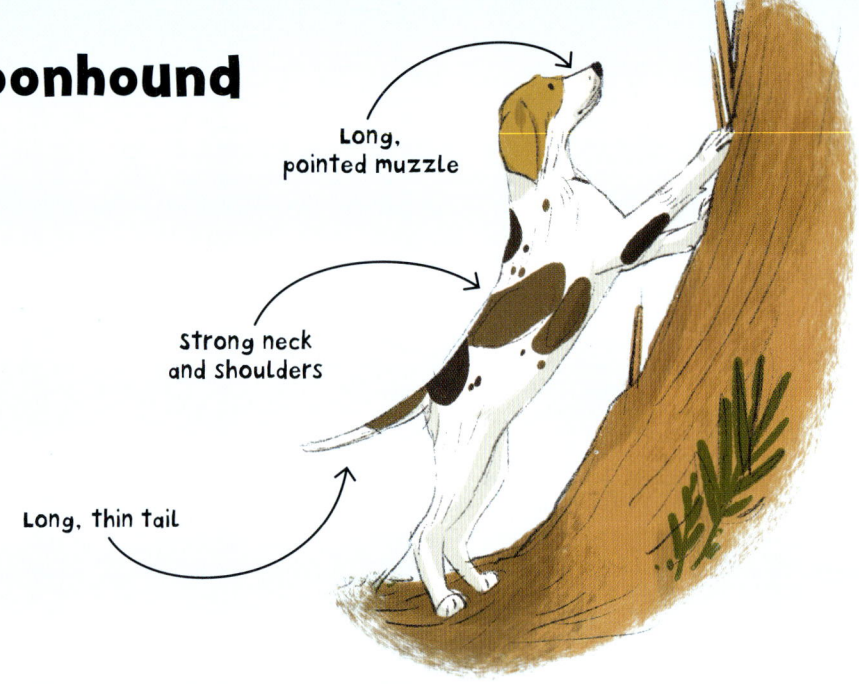

Long, pointed muzzle

Strong neck and shoulders

Long, thin tail

ORIGIN: USA
COAT: Short, smooth
PERSONALITY: Confident and loving

INTELLIGENCE
ENERGY LEVEL
TRAINABILITY

Catahoula Leopard Dog

The state dog of Louisiana is multi-talented. Skilled as both a hunter and a herder, they also have a special talent for climbing trees.

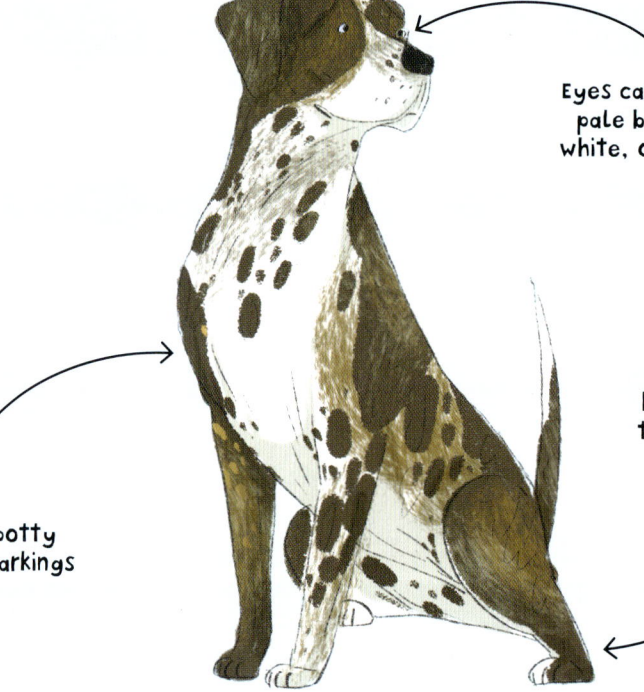

Eyes can be brown, pale blue, grey, white, or a mixture

Their webbed feet help them to paddle through swamps, and to climb trees

Unusual, spotty "Leopard" markings

ORIGIN: USA
COAT: Short, smooth
PERSONALITY: Independent & protective

INTELLIGENCE
ENERGY LEVEL
TRAINABILITY

CLEVER CLIMBERS 23

Norwegian Lundehund

One of the rarest dogs in the world, the Norwegian lundehund was once used to hunt **puffins**. They would have to climb difficult and dangerous cliffs, in search of nests. Thanks to some very unusual physical features, these dogs make incredible rock climbers.

"Elastic" neck can bend all the way back to touch the spine

An extra toe on each foot to help grip rocks

ORIGIN: Norway

COAT: Short, thick

PERSONALITY: Alert and cheerful

INTELLIGENCE 🐾🐾🐾
ENERGY LEVEL 🐾🐾🐾
TRAINABILITY 🐾🐾🐾

Ears can fold shut to protect from dirt and pests

Flexible front legs can stretch all the way out from the body

WHAT'S THAT DOG?

Now that you have read all about super talented dogs, how good are you at identifying them? There are 25 different dogs to figure out. Use the information in the book to help you.

1

What am I?
A. Wire Fox Terrier
B. Border Terrier
C. Nova Scotia Duck Tolling Retriever

2

What am I?
A. Jack Russell Terrier
B. Beagle
C. Border Terrier

3

What am I?
A. Vizsla
B. German Pointer
C. Weimaraner

4

What am I?
A. Norweigan Lundehund
B. English Springer Spaniel
C. Scottish Terrier

5

What am I?
A. Beagle
B. Basset Hound
C. Bluetick Coonhound

6

What am I?
A. Otterhound
B. Weimaraner
C. Catahoula Leopard Dog

7

What am I?
A. Greyhound
B. Lagotto Romagnolo
C. Bloodhound

8

What am I?
A. West Highland White Terrier
B. American Foxhound
C. English Springer Spaniel

9

What am I?
A. Otterhound
B. Saluki
C. Belgian Malinois

10

What am I?
A. Bloodhound
B. Beagle
C. Basset Hound

11

What am I?
A. Portuguese Water Dog
B. Belgian Malinois
C. Whippet

12

What am I?
A. Scottish Terrier
B. Old English Sheepdog
C. Lagotto Romagnolo

13

What am I?
A. Otterhound
B. Whippet
C. Vizsla

Answers can be found on page 32.

14

What am I?
A. Border Terrier
B. Wire Fox Terrier
C. Jack Russell Terrier

15

What am I?
A. Lagotto Romagnolo
B. Weimaraner
C. Bloodhound

16

What am I?
A. Belgian Malinois
B. Whippet
C. Otterhound

17

What am I?
A. Vizsla
B. Scottish Terrier
C. German Pointer

18

What am I?
A. Saluki
B. Greyhound
C. Vizsla

19

What am I?
A. Greyhound
B. Bluetick Coonhound
C. Belgian Malinois

20

What am I?
A. Norwegian Lundehund
B. West Highland White Terrier
C. Border Terrier

21

What am I?
A. Beagle
B. American Foxhound
C. Wire Fox Terrier

22

What am I?
A. Treeing Walker Coonhound
B. Vizsla
C. Portuguese Water Dog

23

What am I?
A. Catahoula Leopard Dog
B. Wire Fox Terrier
C. German Pointer

24

What am I?
A. Jack Russell Terrier
B. Nova Scotia Duck Tolling Retriever
C. Bluetick Coonhound

25

What am I?
A. Portuguese Water Dog
B. Saluki
C. German Pointer

SPOT THE DOG

There are so many brilliant dogs in the world. You can see them everywhere you go: in towns, parks, and sometimes even at the beach! See which of these are the most popular dogs where you live, make a note of them in a notebook if you do spot them.

Vizsla **Whippet** **American Foxhound**

Bloodhound **Saluki** **Belgian Malinois**

Which dogs do you think will be the most and least common in your area? Write your guesses in a notebook and check if you were right. You may be suprised how many you spot, now that you know your breeds!

Greyhound

Bluetick Coonhound

West Highland White Terrier

Beagle

Scottish Terrier

Lagotto Romagnolo

Have you spotted me when you're out-and-about?

Have you seen me before?

Border Terrier

Jack Russell Terrier

German Pointer

Wire Fox Terrier

English Springer Spaniel

Norwegian Lundehund

SKILLS TO THE TEST

We have seen how many dogs are super talented, but how do they use these skills in real life? Take a look at these amazing stories from some of the world's cleverest dogs.

Medical Emergency

Many scent hounds look after owners with specific medical conditions. They can smell the chemical changes before the person passes out or becomes very ill, and can warn them or bring them medication.

An assistant dog goes with their owner everywhere, to make sure they can sense any changes before they happen.

Dogs can also help with allergies. Some dogs, such as vizslas, are trained to sniff out nuts in food. They alert their owners to the nuts by sitting between them and the food, and refusing to budge. These dogs save lives every day.

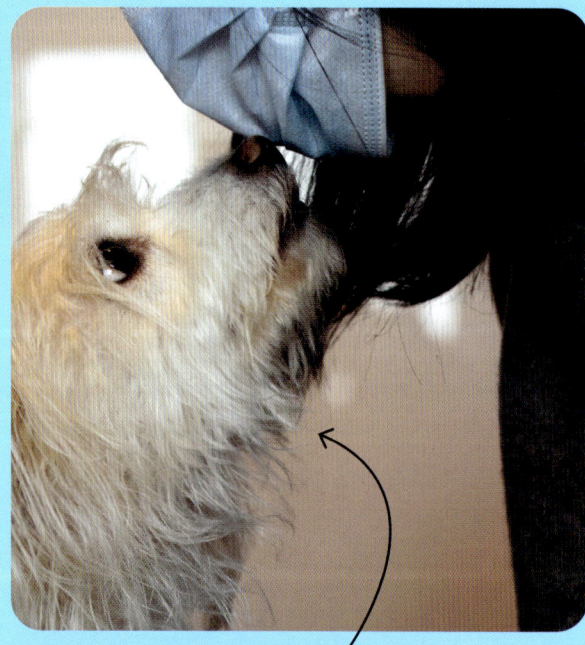

Dogs can even be trained to sniff out diseases in living people, such as cancer and COVID-19. It requires months and months of training, but some dogs are more accurate than scientific tests for these diseases. How amazing is that?

Police Sidekicks

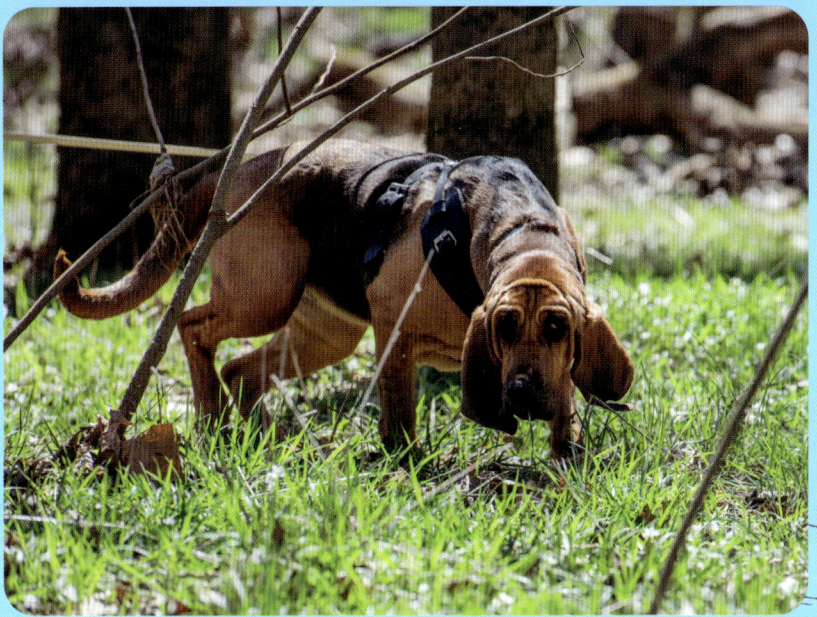

Dogs have helped the police and solved cases for hundreds of years. One of the most successful police dogs is Radar, a bloodhound from the USA, who has helped solve 24 murder cases and assisted in lots more! He uses his super sensitive nose to sniff out evidence, suspects, and even missing people.

Bloodhounds help with police investigations by tracking with their super noses!

Military Lifesavers

Patron proves that dogs can do anything they put their mind – or nose – to. This Jack Russell terrier helped the Ukraine military to detect explosives that even metal detectors missed! Military detection is usually the job for German Shepherds and Labradors, but because Patron is smaller and lighter, he can go where bigger dogs can't. He detected over 200 explosives in total!

GLOSSARY

Adopting – Legally taking on the animal as your own, receiving all responsibility.

Agility (dog sport) – a sport where dogs complete complicated obstacle courses, including objects that they have run through, around, under, or jump over.

Burrows – holes or tunnels dug by animals.

Characteristics – a feature or quality of a person, place, or thing.

Descendants – people or animals that are related to an individual or group who lived in the past. For example, you are a descendant of your parents and grandparents.

Detection dogs – dogs that are trained to use their senses (usually smell) to detect items, such as explosives and illegal drugs. They are also known as sniffer dogs.

Domesticate – to be tamed or trained to live or work with humans.

Puffins – black and white seabirds that nest in holes and caves along coastal cliffs.

Rehoming shelter – a place where dogs (or other animals) who were lost, stray, or given up by their owners, are looked after until they can be adopted into a new home.

Therapy dog – dogs that are trained to provide comfort and support to people. Unlike service dogs who only assist one person, therapy dogs help multiple individuals, or groups of people. They often work in hospitals, schools, or nursing and retirement homes.

Truffle – a strong-smelling edible fungus that grows underground. They are expensive because they are very rare.

Wiry – a type of dog coat that is rough, thick, and bristly.

INDEX

A
American foxhound 10, 26

B
basset hound 10
beagle 12, 27
Belgian Malinois 13, 26
bloodhound 8-9, 10, 26, 29
bluetick coonhound 12, 27
border terrier 19, 27

C
Catahoula leopard dog 22

E
English springer spaniel 11, 27

G
German pointer 21, 27
greyhound 14-15, 16-17, 27

H
herding breed group 7
hound breed group 7, 9, 10-11, 12-13, 14-15, 16-17, 22, 26-27

J
Jack Russell terrier 17, 27, 29

L
Lagotto Romagnolo 13, 27

N
non-sporting breed group 6
Norwegian lundehund 23, 27
Nova Scotia duck tolling retriever 21

O
otterhound 11

P
Portuguese water dog 20

S
saluki 16, 26
scent hound 7, 8-9, 10-11, 12-13, 26-27, 28-29
Scottish terrier 18, 27
sighthound 7, 14-15, 16-17, 26-27
sporting breed group 6

T
terrier 6, 17, 18-19, 26-27, 29
toy breed group 7
treeing walker coonhound 22

V
vizsla 16, 26, 28

W
Weimaraner 20
West Highland white terrier 18, 27
wire fox terrier 19, 27
whippet 17, 26
working breed group 6

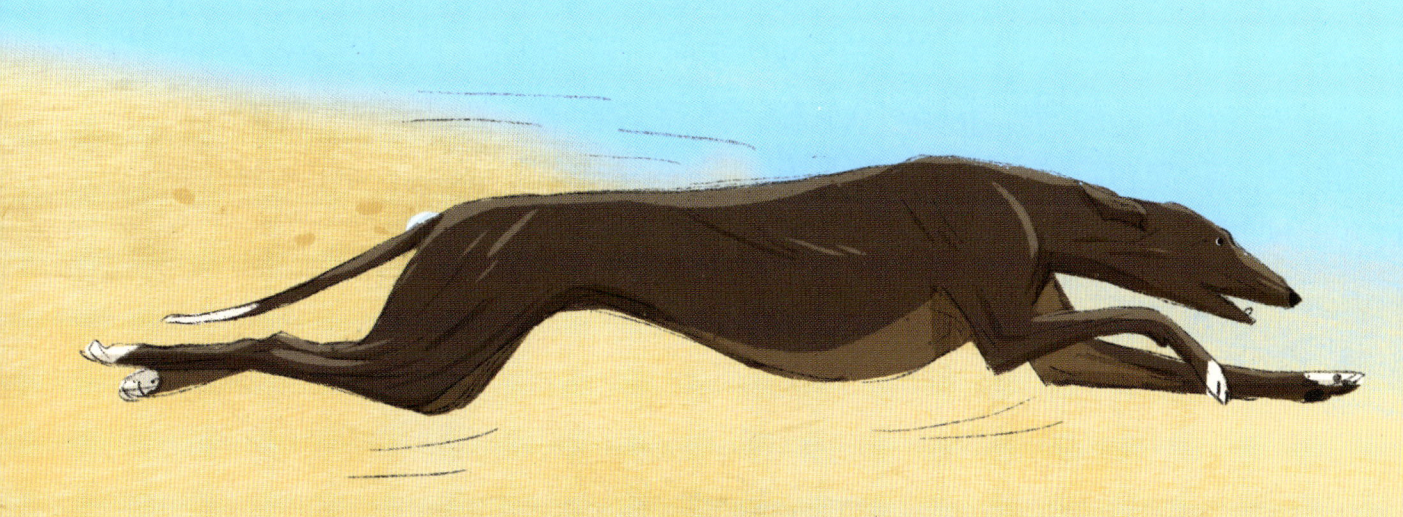

WHAT'S THAT DOG ANSWERS

1 - B. Border Terrier
2 - A. Jack Russell Terrier
3 - C. Weimaraner
4 - A. Norwegian Lundehund
5 - A. Beagle
6 - A. Otterhound
7 - B. Lagotto Romagnolo
8 - C. English Springer Spaniel
9 - B. Saluki
10 - C. Basset Hound
11 - A. Portuguese Water Dog
12 - A. Scottish Terrier
13 - B. Whippet
14 - B. Wire Fox Terrier
15 - C. Bloodhound
16 - A. Belgian Malinois
17 - A. Vizsla
18 - B. Greyhound
19 - B. Bluetick Coonhound
20 - B. West Highland White Terrier
21 - B. American Foxhound
22 - A. Treeing Walker Coonhound
23 - A. Catahoula Leopard Dog
24 - B. Nova Scotia Duck Tolling Retriever
25 - C. German Pointer

ABOUT THE AUTHOR

Annabel is a writer and artist based in London, UK. Having worked as a bookseller for many years, she now writes children's books focusing on animals and the natural world. Her recent titles include *What Can I See in the Wild?*, *Seasons* and *The Spectacular Lives of Sharks*.

ABOUT THE ILLUSTRATOR

Marina is a talented illustrator of children's books from Ukraine. Her stunning illustrations are inspired by her own childhood, children, nature, magical moments and fairytales.

Picture Credits:
(abbreviations: t=top, b=bottom, m=middle, l=left, r=right)

Alexey Androsov 24ml, 27ml; Aneta Placha 25bmr; DragoNika 24tmr; EMT100 25m, 27tr; Eve Photography 24br, 24mbr, 27m; Hector Rivera Casillas 25ml, 27tl; L i g h t p o e t 24tl, 27bml; Lars Christensen 24tl, 27br; Liudmila Bohush 25tr, 26tl; Lourdes Photography 24m; Mariana Campos Carretero 25tml, 26ml; Martin Christopher Parker 24mr, 27bm; Mary Kolesnik 24bml; Mary Swift 25bl, 25m, 25mr, 26tr, 27tm; Nik174 25t, 26tm; NSC Photography 29tl; Otsphoto 25bl; Rfranca 28br; Ricantimages 24m, 27mr; Smit 24tm, 27bm; Susan B Sheldon 28tl; Thka 29br; TSViPhoto 25tl, 27bl; Victoria Antonova 25tmr, 26mr; Vitalii_Mamchuk 25br, 27mr; Xkunclova 24bl, 26m.

Every effort has been made to trace the copyright holders, and we apologise in advance for any unintentional omissions. We would be pleased to insert the appropriate acknowledgements in any subsequent edition of this publication.